Praise for *The Taste of Ambiance*

"When creating our custom wine cellars for our home, Al and Dragon Cellars were able to bring our vision to life. From the custom humidor to the unique display of our collection, there was no detail overlooked. Thank you, Al!"

—DJ Khaled and Family

"I greatly value the care of wine, being a sommelier, to ensure that it is maintained properly with the right temperature and conditions. Al has always kept these critical factors in mind while designing the most spectacular cellars. This book is a great representation of many of his works of art."

—Javier Gila, Five-Time Winner of the "Best Sommelier in Spain" Title, Finalist in World Sommelier Championship and European Championship in 2000

"The importance of good storage to allow wines to develop and avoid potential problems cannot be overstated. Collectors also like their cellars to be showcases. There are certainly some delightful wine cellars in *The Taste of Ambiance*, which is sure to appeal to any wine enthusiast."

—Keith Grainger, Founding Member of the Association of Wine Educators, Gourmand Award-Winner for "Best Wine Book in the World for Professionals in Twenty-Five Years," and Author of *Wine Faults and Flaws: A Practical Guide*

"*The Taste of Ambience* is a Powerball jackpot fantasy for the oenophile. Al Fuentes has created fabulous pajamas in which fine wines will sleep until summoned to their purpose."

—Willie Reale, Emmy Award-Winner, MacArthur Fellow, and Founding Member of the New York Wine Club

"It gives me great pleasure to provide my comments on Al Fuentes' book, a complete collection of his works of art relating to the care and display of wine. It is very gratifying to highlight that our wine cellar is part of this. We observe with gratitude the ambiance that is generated in El Bohio thanks to this project and literary contribution."

—Pepe Rodríguez Rey, Michelin-Rated Chef and Owner of El Bohio (Restaurant in Toledo, Spain), and Ten-Year *MasterChef* Judge

"Uncork the secrets of wine enjoyment with this beautifully crafted guide. From the grandeur of meticulously designed wine cellars to the intimate corners of wine-bar rooms, this book is a treasure trove of ideas for anyone aspiring to bring the soul of vineyards into their home and artfully blend the elegance of wine-related furniture and the charm of specialized wine rooms. It's not just a book; it's a gateway to a lifestyle where every sip tells a story!"

—Lynette Janac, Editor-in-Chief/CEO, *Luxury Guide USA*

"It has been a pleasure to work with Al in designing our restaurant cellar where our wine is clearly displayed and well organized. We have received rave reviews from our customers and various awards related to our vast list of great wines. This book is very effective to show off what he is capable of, and his comments on this subject are spot-on!"

—Raúl Barroso, Owner of Asador Las Esparteras (Restaurant in Toledo, Spain), Selected by Wine Challenge Merchant Awards Spain 2022 for "Top Three Restaurant Wine List," and Recipient of the Repsol Guide Sun Award for Wine Cellar

"Our exclusive wine room created by Dragon Cellars met all the requirements we needed for our restaurant, BiBo, in Madrid. It was designed to hold great wine, and its impeccable operation has guaranteed the perfect care of our bottles. This wine cellar was a key milestone that highlighted the before and after of the Dani García group. Congratulations for so much creativity reflected in this outstanding book."

—Laura Gutiérrez, Partner of the Dani García Group and Michelin-Rated Chef

"Al Fuentes's masterful designs with respect to space and aesthetic is beautifully displayed in *The Taste of Ambiance: Luxury Wine Cellar Designs*. Al delicately captures a window into the soul of a wine collector. My mind wanders into oblivion as I imagine the future wine cellar space I will commission Al to design for me."

—Matthew Kaner, Wine Director, Educator, and Owner of Will Travel For Wine Inc., Sommelier, and Wine Correspondent for *Men's Journal*

"Al's book is a must-have for the wine connoisseur, showing his unique, custom wine cellar and designs. Besides the numerous quality photos, he educates us on different aspects of these wine-care and display projects. Definitely a coffee table book I will have at home next to the beautiful modern cellar he created for me!"

—Mark Moses, CEO and Founding Partner of Coaching International, Bestselling Author of *Make BIG Happen* and *Making BIG Happen*

"Al Fuentes created works of art for two of our restaurants to display and care for our wine; clients loved them. I congratulate him on developing this very complete book of beautiful residential and commercial wine cellars and am glad to see my photos are included. I will definitely have a copy on hand in a privileged location."

—Anxo Garcia, Amicalia Galician Hospitality Group, Owners of Previous Michelin Star Restaurant, Alborada

"Al Fuentes turns traditional wine cellars inside out. He puts the bottles themselves on full display, making them the principal design element in his glass-enclosed showcases. His work is handsome and impressive—and will make readers want to pull a cork."

—Peter Herdrich, CEO of Cultural Capital Group, LLC and Executive Director of New York Wine Club

"Immerse yourself in these stunning displays of wine rooms and walls, beautifully captured in this book to inspire and elevate your appreciation for the art of wine. A must-have for enthusiasts and connoisseurs alike."

—Nina Marco, Interior Designer of Casa de Marco Design

"The care for the design, the quality of production, and the attention to detail of all critical technical demands highlights each wine bottle as if it were a jewel. *The Taste of Ambiance* explains the Dragon Cellars process and enchants us with numerous photos and renders of their masterpieces for all to enjoy. I love it!"

—Arturo Berned, Award-Winning Spanish Sculptor

The Taste of Ambiance

The TASTE of AMBIANCE

LUXURY WINE CELLAR DESIGNS

AL FUENTES

BROWN BOOKS
PUBLISHING GROUP

The Taste of Ambiance: Luxury Wine Cellar Designs

Brown Books Publishing Group
Dallas, TX / New York, NY
www.BrownBooks.com
(972) 381-0009

A New Era in Publishing®

Publisher's Cataloging-In-Publication Data

Names: Fuentes, Al, author.
Title: The taste of ambiance : luxury wine cellar designs / Al Fuentes.
Description: Dallas, TX ; New York, NY : Brown Books Publishing Group, [2024]
Identifiers: ISBN: 978-1-61254-678-0 (hardcover) | LCCN: 2023949674
Subjects: LCSH: Wine cellars--Designs and plans. | Dwellings--Design and construction. | Wine-- Storage. | BISAC: COOKING / Beverages / Alcoholic / Wine. | HOUSE & HOME / Design & Construction. | HOUSE & HOME / Decorating & Furnishings.
Classification: LCC: TP548.5.A6 F84 2024 | DDC: 641.22--dc23

ISBN 978-1-61254-678-0
LCCN 2023949674

Printed in China
10 9 8 7 6 5 4 3 2 1

Photo Credit: Artefacto, pages 3, 82, 88–9

For more information or to contact the author, please go to www.TasteOfAmbiance.com.

I happily dedicate this book to two of my most important family members and supporters of the Dragon Cellars business. Without them, the success we have would have been impossible.

Firstly, my mother, Josefa Figueirido, who passed away just a few years ago at the ripe age of ninety-nine. Her loving care, guidance, and support of my creativity were key in my ability to design and think "outside the box." Her constant encouragement and financial support were crucial to help get the company on the right track and spring forward during troubling times.

Secondly is my wife, Marisol Lecuna, who is mentioned in the book as our general manager. From day one she believed in me and in the business, assisting in all key areas. Eventually she joined the team and was the main factor is promoting Dragon Cellars to begin operations in the United States. Her expert opinion and contributions in most of the critical departments of the company has led to our market leadership.

I'm sure both of these lovely women are very proud of what we have achieved, and since this book is a small reflection of our accomplishments, it is dedicated to them.

HINE
RARE
BASIL HAYDEN'S
EL DORADO
BLACK LABEL
Old Parr
12
RED DRUM
BOURBON WHISKEY
BRAULIO
WIDOW JANE
AGED 10 YEARS
LEOPOLD BROS
WHISTLEPIG
HORSE SOLDIER
VODKA
Tito's
Handmade
CK
GAS

Contents

Foreword

I met my friend Al Fuentes at the start of this century when he was working as an associate professor for Schiller International University. At the time, he was already an oenophile interested in quality wines and everything related to this wonderful world. He was an avid participant in courses and wine tasting that the Spanish Association of Wine Tasters (Union Española de Catadores) organized. His keen interest in the selection of premium wines and all the necessary conditions to care for them until they reach their maturity was a clear sign of how he would focus his future.

One of the most important key elements for a wine lover or collector is constructing a quality cellar where an owner can care for their "treasure." This special place must have the ideal conditions to conserve wine and ensure it evolves optimally through its complete life cycle so it can be enjoyed at all its stages. I can say that, for me, this is the first and most important factor to keep in mind relative to the storage of our precious wine.

Wine is not only a food, but a living entity that changes throughout its life. It can evolve while maintaining its positive characteristics if properly kept but can spoil if not cared for. A good wine with capacity to mature and evolve will express in its first year's strength and fruitiness, smoothing out and balancing with time, becoming more expressive and complex. This is why it's so appealing to store bottles of a very good vintage and enjoy it as it evolves.

In order to store wine, it is not sufficient to simply keep it in a cabinet and wait for time to pass. Factors such as constant temperature between 56°F–59°F and a relative humidity around 60 to 75 percent are a guarantee that we will be able to drink our wines in their moment of maximum expression.

Through his company, Dragon Cellars, Al has seen this important opportunity in the wine industry, not only providing care for the wine but also making this space stand out in a home or restaurant. He uses the best quality materials as well as the most innovative designs. The attention to detail of these factors takes into consideration the location where the wine cellar/wall will be located and what modern materials—such as metal, glass, and acrylic—are used, which contrast the more impersonal and antiquated wood racking and cabinetry. To enhance his projects, Al uses LED lighting for ambiance that does not affect how the wine is cared for but highlights these "works of art." His solutions have the combination of being aesthetic while also functional, and results in being the focal point in the home or restaurant, giving emphasis to the displayed "treasures."

The success of Al Fuentes and Dragon Cellars is clearly seen with the market leadership he has attained over these years, and is accompanied by his international operations. He has done business in seven countries, with offices in Delray Beach (southeast Florida) and Madrid (Spain, Iberian Peninsula). With his bilingual English and Spanish capabilities, he serves clientele in the US market, Spain, and the Caribbean as well. The manufacturing capability is located in Madrid, where all the racking, cabinets, and wine-related furniture are produced. His projects are located in high-end homes and very renowned restaurants, including Michelin-rated.

I hope you enjoy this book and keep your precious wines displayed and cared for in spaces designed and customized by Al and Dragon Cellars. If that's not possible, then drink your wine quickly and enjoy it while it's "alive." Save the empty bottles as mementos.

—Fernando Gurucharri Jaque,
President of Spanish Association of Wine Tasters
(Presidente de Unión Española de Catadores)

Introduction

The Taste of Ambiance is a visual representation of close to seventeen years of trying to make a difference in the storage, display, and care of wine. Dragon Cellars's mission is to provide innovative and stunning-looking wine cellars as well as the catered places built for enjoying wine in all types of establishments, even where underground options are not possible. Although it is a privilege to have an underground space where cool, stable temperature exists with the right amount of humidity and no equipment needed (passive cellar), in many places this is not possible. If a basement is not viable or you live in a condo, you have to find ways of placing these cellars strategically in the home or restaurant where they "show off" the wine and create a totally unique ambiance.

Our foresight has led us to change the paradigm of what has been the standard for cellars for many decades, evolving from, "Nice," to, "Wow." From functional to aesthetics. From being underground to being seen in the dining or living room. From modular wood racks to custom racks in any material imaginable. As the first and only 100 percent custom design and manufacturing company that creates new wine racks in metal, acrylic, stone, glass, and wood—all integrated and tailored to each project—our personalized solution focus was applied to clients in seven countries, making construction that more challenging.

In doing so, I have learned a great deal about the display, care, and personal preferences of hundreds of customers. There is no one "right" way to do any of this; most importantly, it is vital to listen to what the owners want. Some technical aspects of wine care may vary if, for example, you are a more conservative collector. Or perhaps if your wine inventory is quite modest, you have an important rotation of your stock. Your taste in having a wine-cellar design be more modern, more transitional, or traditional is completely up to you, but it is our responsibility to make this custom solution fit your needs. Our focus, through Dragon Cellars, is to act as a consultant as well as a designer.

All of the images displayed in this book are a result of extensive work with each client. There are a variety of finishes, materials, wine organization, and display-rack configurations, but what they all have in common is the importance we give to the lighting effect. I have always said that if your wine cellar/room/wall is not lit, it virtually does not exist. Your guests may not even notice it's there. Dragon Cellars is known for always providing a wine-care solution with aesthetics being a focal point. If this latter factor is not important to the owner, which is respectable, our services might not be valued sufficiently enough to warrant contracting us for the job.

My previous background in headhunting, teaching, and aircraft maintenance has nothing to do with wine cellars. However, my focus on service and my endeavor to both enjoy life and help others do the same is making this phase of my life extremely satisfying. The enthusiasm shown by the owners for the end result, be it residential or commercial, is its very own reward. To be able to contemplate a beautiful wine display and care for a project from its initial concept to its development and installation is exhilarating. This book's purpose is to fill a void in the market: providing an emphasis on modern and transitional styles of custom wine cellars alongside some informative notes on each project, giving options for different styles that has yet to be done. Each page has riveting and personalized features that help differentiate the overall look from any other.

These above-ground wine cellars in modern and transitional styles are my contribution to the world of custom wine cellar designs. I sincerely hope you enjoy this book and appreciate reading about our projects as much as our team enjoyed bringing them to life.

3705
17"
2842
2399.
4293
635.

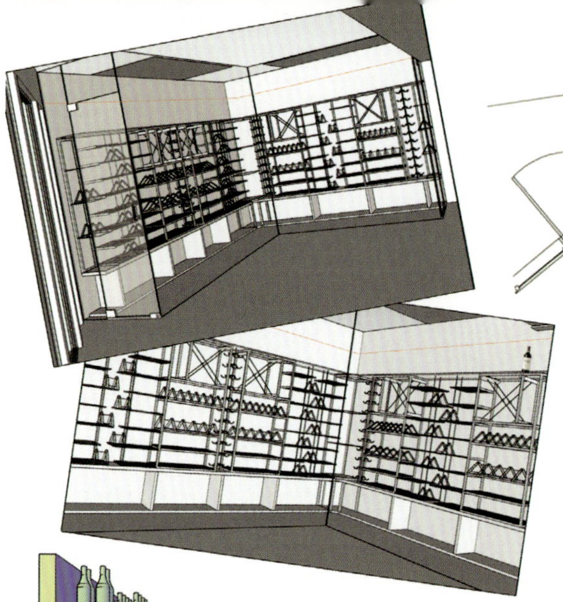

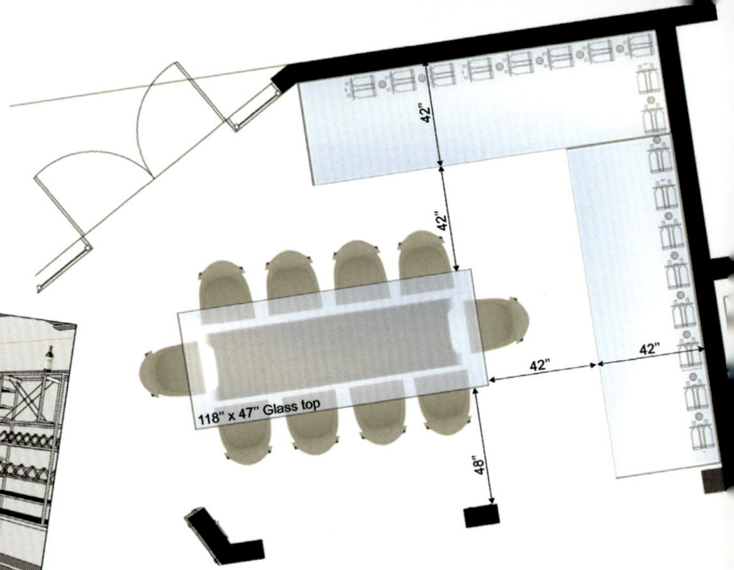
42"
42"
42"
42"
118" x 47" Glass top
48"

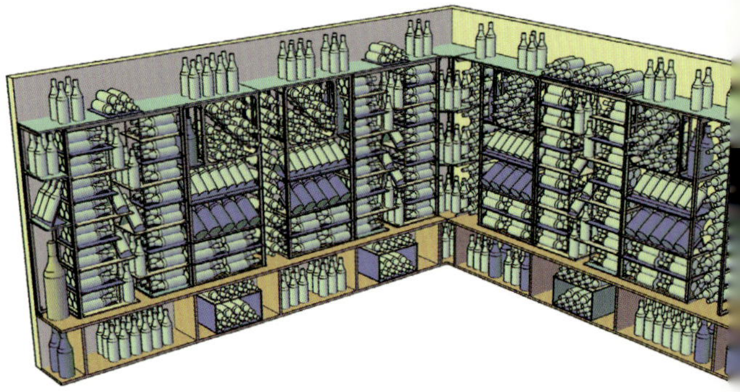

Before, During, and After

It's amazing how a space can transform itself from either being unused or differently purposed to becoming an elegant wine room or wall. There is a lot of work involved in achieving the end goal of a work-of-art project for both the care and display of wine. The main phases involved are:

1. **Designing.** With the dimensions available, and with the owner's feedback as well as their "look" intent, the space can now be designed. Wine organization, materials, finishes, and visual effect are all taken into consideration.

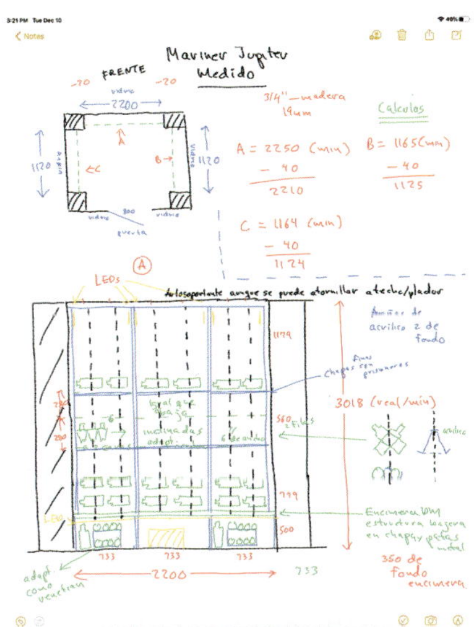

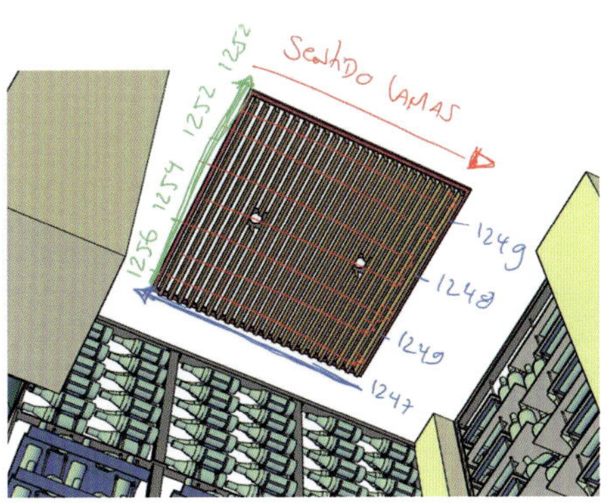

2. **Construction.** This part is always simpler when it's a new home being built. If it is not, then demolition will most likely be required to open up the walls and ceiling. Proper space preparation will be needed to condition the area to hold the proper temperature. The enclosure will also be key in providing a visual "window" to the inside.

3. **Assembly.** With the space readied, the selected custom racking with lights is installed and the cooling system is tested to ensure correct conservation temperature and relative humidity. Wine can now be stocked.

4. **Enjoyment.** With wine in place and the room or wall lit up, it is now the moment to make this focal point in the home stand out. It not only should act as an attention grabber but as the perfect accompaniment to experience wine at its fullest in the ideal ambiance.

Diversity of Styles

There are many ways to display and store wine with a variety of looks, materials, and finishes. For the purpose of simplicity, we will focus on two styles which are the most common: modern and transitional. Regardless of what category may apply to your space or what the wine cellar is designated as, the importance in most cases is that the cellar integrates well with the mood and décor of the rest of the house or restaurant.

Modern Style

Wine display and storage solutions that are considered modern are more and more prevalent in today's projects. Homes are lighter and more minimalistic with simpler, elegant lines. Therefore, these wine cellars must follow suit. It is more frequent to use metal racking, steel cables, glass shelving, acrylic pieces, and lacquered wood that provides a clean look and gives more emphasis to the wine itself. Often, clients and designers request to have a wine-racking system (or systems) where the bottles seem to float in place. Thinner materials and lighter colored elements will provide a perfect contrast to red wine bottles and help tremendously with the reflection of LED lighting, resulting in a breathtaking ambiance.

Transitional Style

This is a design category used in wine cellars and walls that combines the use of lighter materials with warm finishes. Wine is placed on elements that are not so thick, such as typical wood. The wood that is used can be leaner with a lighter washed look to make the grain stand out as a natural product but is accompanied by several metal pieces that can be lacquered in any tone. Some stainless steel can even be incorporated for elegance. To result in a less bulky look, the racking modules can be placed without added wooden backing. Having these racks open and the walls either painted or finished in a lighter color will allow the bottles to have a nice contrast and better reflect the placed lighting, which can be warm white or amber.

Wine-Related Furniture

In order to complement a wine cellar or room, cabinetry and furniture can be very useful to the homeowner so that they can better delight in this experience. Besides having racking to store and display wine, you will need additional places for helpful accoutrements. Cabinets can be made where both wine glasses can be stored and drawers are places for accessories, such as cork screws. These cabinets can also store items that you want either hidden or visible, like beautiful decanters. Lighted tasting counters or tables are a perfect place to have a correct visual tasting to check in on how the wine is oxidizing. You can perform your opening and enjoyment either by standing or using the table and chairs/stools for a relaxed, sit-down experience. Often, custom cigar humidors made with the same outside material and finish are integrated into these spaces. In this case, the proper temperature and humidity control must be considered. It's always impressive if these pieces are lit just like the surrounding wine racking system for that impressionable effect. In this furniture category, you can include custom bars that also hold wine fridges that keep white or sparkling wine at just the right serving temperature. To keep with the same aesthetics, the commercial fridges can use the same finish on their panel-ready pieces, or you can simply manufacture a custom refrigerated cabinet with the racks and lighting to match the rest of the area.

Wine-Enjoyment Area

Throughout the years, basic care for wine has been at the forefront when wine cellars or rooms have been constructed. The tendency to situate these special bottles closer to where they will be drunk and provide an aesthetic focal point in the home is becoming more prevalent. Once you have a beautiful place that creates a unique ambiance, the ideal scenario is to be able to enjoy the wine next to this element. Therefore, the experiential factor emerges so that the room or area provides a more complete fulfillment of the wine.

With this focus, the tasks of selecting, opening, tasting, decanting, and drinking wine with family and friends makes for a prime environment to share in. To realize all these experiences, we need to ensure that, besides having a place to care for and display wine, you also have the furniture pieces available that are needed, such as: accessory storage, glass holders, lighted tasting counters, decanter shelving, and the proper seating arrangement to accompany this experience. The space can be as formal or casual as you desire, with sofa seats or a counter-height table and stools. The end product is a wine-enjoyment area that focuses on wine separate from a bar area.

Residential Projects

There has been a clear and increasing demand for the placement of wine care and display areas in private homes. The traditional underground and dark wine cellar has gone from just keeping wine for proper aging and future consumption at the right conditions (temperature and humidity) to an element that involves it being featured in a more prominent place in the home. This new focus allows the wine to be closer to where it is consumed and provides both an ambiance and visual effect that fulfills the complete wine-enjoyment escapade.

Not only are these focal points placed in houses, but more often than not, they're in condos. Often referred to as wine cellars still, these rooms and walls tend to be focused on displaying or storing for a shorter period. Many times, owners involve interior designers to ensure that the materials and finishes integrate perfectly with the look of the home. The client mostly provides feedback on how they would like the bottles to be placed and organized. The company that attends to them should act as a consultant to ensure that the final product is the functional and aesthetic solution that the client needs.

There are types of clients that value different features for their "wine cellar." It may vary from having "unbothered" wine in a dark room with the right climate conditions to a glass-enclosed, wine-display room—and even a lit wall in the center of the living or dining room. In some instances, the owner will prefer to have this key design element in their home without cooling since the wine will not be stored for long and has a high rotation. This concept is complemented with a wine fridge in the case of having higher-end bottles as well as for being able to keep whites and champagne at serving temperature. Depending on the owner's profile, various options are available.

Homes

Single-family homes that have an adequate space—be it in a basement or ground level—are the ideal location to place and properly condition a wine cellar/room/wall. Some lucky owners have a properly cooled and humidity-controlled environment in their basement that is stable year-round, so no equipment expenses are needed. When basements are not an option, such as in Florida, the walls and ceiling have to be prepared so that they can maintain the right conditions. When some of these walls have glass sides, then the equipment needs to be sized correctly to compensate. In any case, the evolution of these wine-care-and-display solutions are becoming more aesthetic with the best possible view of the wine, primarily in the living- and dining-room areas. The special ambiance created becomes more and more relevant compared to having the wine hidden away in a dark, enclosed room. These spaces tend to be larger than those placed in condos.

Condos

Wine rooms and walls are being placed more often in condos. Many times these relatively "small" living spaces still have owners that love both wine and entertaining. On many occasions, these condos may be a second or seasonal home. The need for them is still valid, but they do tend to be smaller in size. In any case, they present a technical challenge that, at times, results in the project being discarded. Cooling systems that require special installations, HOA and city approvals, construction work, etc., make these jobs costly and lengthy in time. These projects normally utilize various glass walls and tend to be contemporary. The racking is designed for being minimalistic with steel, glass, acrylic, and solid-colored wood and is accompanied with the proper LED lighting so that the view provides a stunning glow. On several occasions, the custom refrigerated wine cabinets with the finishes that match the home décor light up in order to show the wine labels, only requiring to be plugged in. These are always a great option.

RATPACK

Modern Home Projects

Barnsley Wine Room and Bar

Parkland, Florida

Showcased is the total solution of an enclosed, refrigerated wine room with modern gray-tone finishes that uses metal, acrylic, and wood elements. It is a dynamic display and a varied organization of wine. Just outside a medium-density fiberboard (MDF), lacquered, lighted tasting counter is a white-wine fridge with glass shelving and cabinetry for varied storage. Beautiful stone and LEDs for lighting create a unique ambiance for peak enjoyment.

Boca East Wine Room and Bar

Boca Raton, Florida

This glass-enclosed corner wine room is a focal point in the home to display wine and enjoy a tasting. A serving bar with a glass holder is next to the window. Light materials like glass, acrylic, and thin metal are used to focus on transparency and permit a better reflection of the changing LED lights. Warmth is also transmitted from wood elements, such as the counter, bottom cabinets, and the technical ceiling.

OVID

Eagle Arched Glass Wine Room

Jupiter, Florida

This one of a kind, extra-transparent wine room display amazes guests from the ground floor when entering the home. Major emphasis is placed on using all acrylic and low-iron glass pieces with very thin, light gray metal to show only the bottles and perfectly reflect the LED lights that are embedded in the framing. This piece is situated on the upper level next to the bar so that wine can be easily accessed, and it creates that exclusive ambiance needed for entertainment.

Chianti Wine Bar

Boca Raton, Florida

Pictured is a glass-enclosed corner wine room that is the first element you see when entering the home. This is a practical area that allows for easily accessible, ready-to-drink wine with a glass holder above and an aesthetic display of bottles on two walls. There is an opening in the glass just above the lighted tasting counter for serving, which also incorporates a cigar humidor. Glass and metal racking permits display of all types of bottles.

Harbor Way Wine Room

Deerfield Beach, Florida

A large, refrigerated wine room for over 2,500 bottles is situated at the entrance of the home. This is a complex and complete project that incorporates light gray metal racking with glass and acrylic and is complemented with a lighted counter, a glass holder, and a centrally situated waterfall table with its stools. The ceiling slats are in the same wood finish as the storage cabinet and completed with backlit blue stone glass. An astonishing ambiance is created inside as well as outside of this matchless room.

Coffee Wine Room

Deerfield Beach, Florida

Shown is the result of a conversion from a bathroom to a glass-enclosed refrigerated wine room. To make the space more open, the corner beam was removed. This creates a unique space to store and display wine and makes the room practical. A lightly lighted tasting counter with upper glass shelving was included to place glasses and decanters. Light-colored metal racking with glass and lacquered wood was added as well as RGB LED lighting.

Glen Understairs Wine Room

Doral, Florida

A complete conversion has transformed an understairs closet to this elegant open wine room. The front and side walls open up for the glass and for a clear view of the wine. Light gray metal racks with cables and acrylic hooks as well as a narrow metal-and-glass counter allows for a display of bottles, showcased in various formats. Back space has also been utilized for added neck-out storage. LEDs and high hat lights make this job a work of art and give it an astonishing look.

Venetian Wine Room and Counter

Venetian Islands, Florida

An elegant wine room with a glass enclosure wraps around two walls, providing the perfect aura for this dining room. A combination of metal, cables, and acrylic shelving allows for an impressive organization and display of wine. The bottom cabinet is ideal for crates and magnums. Outside, in between two columns, a lighted counter with a glass holder serves as a stage to open, decant, and taste wine.

SILVER OAK CELLARS

Vintage Wine and Spirits Room and Bar

Palm Beach Gardens, Florida

A refrigerated and glass-enclosed space allows the living room and kitchen to be separated utilizing this element. Bottles are displayed with labels visible from two sides by using acrylic and cables. Placed against the wall are spirits with alternating glass shelves on top of a lacquered MDF cabinet. Just outside is a lighted counter with shelves, a glass holder, and stools that provide service in entertaining guests. RGB LED lights are lit within.

Enclave Wine Display Room

Boca Raton, Florida

A tall, unrefrigerated wine room has been placed on a main wall in the living room. The "spider" design used allows wine to be displayed in transparent shelving and racking. Walk-in space allows the glass front to be totally clean with the side door. Added stylish features include a custom ladder, a lighted counter, a cigar humidor, a glass holder, and upper display shelves for large formats.

Seasage Wine Room

Delray Beach, Florida

This glass-enclosed wine room was created to have a unique view from the dining room and be accessed from a bar and serving area. The focus was to make all racking elements as light as possible with metal, cables, and acrylic so that the bottles can be displayed in a dynamic fashion. A small tasting counter in the center, wood slat ceiling, and LED lighting give a touch of warmth to this modern setup.

HUNDRED ACRE

Rosella Wine Room

Boca Raton, Florida

The owner conditioned a room to have a refrigerated area to care for his wine while keeping the outside space ventilated to enjoy cigars. The walk-in room has glass from floor to ceiling by housing the cooling unit inside an internal soffit. The enclosure was quite clean, having only one door. The features utilized with the cabinet, humidor, counter, and glass holder makes this area both cool and functional.

Orchid Glass Wine Room

Boca Raton, Florida

This corner space was perfect to place a refrigerated wine room with a glass enclosure and a side door. This structure can be clearly seen upon entering and throughout the home. The two walls have laser-cut racks that can alternate between neck-out or tilted positions by the use of a removable plate. A small glass counter by the front allows special bottles to be highlighted. The RGB LEDs provided an ambiance glow par to none.

Aldama Artistic Wine Room

La Moraleja, Madrid, Spain

This unique wine tasting area contains a backlit onyx waterfall bar and a refrigerated wine room with various artistic glass panels. The wine is placed in metal racking with two special diamond-shaped cable modules and other niches for bottles positioned either neck out or tilted. Corner glass shelves have been used to maximize capacity and place magnums. A functional counter with drawers serves as a perfect opening and staging area.

Collection Suites Understairs Wine Room

Doral, Florida

Shown is a luxury collection suite that takes full advantage of a metal understairs space to display the owner's top-quality wine while utilizing various accompanying works of art and exclusive vehicles. This two-sided walk-in enclosure ensures lightness and transparency by using acrylic, glass, and metal shelving as well as cables. The bottles seem to float and can be properly seen from all angles, especially when lit with the LED lighting that's embedded in the racks.

EXIT

Puerta de Hierro Understairs Wine Room

Madrid, Spain

An understairs closet has been converted to a wine room after extensive construction. The back wall had to obstruct a doorway, whereas the front had to open up enough room to place a window and glass door. A cooling unit is hidden in soffit while an optimized racking layout wraps around three walls to maximize capacity. Two-tone dynamic metal racking provides versatility in organizing and displaying the bottles.

Arrecife Underground Wine Room

Punta Cana, Dominican Republic

A rectangular wine room has racking placed in a U-shaped layout with LEDS to provide a pleasing ambiance. Symmetrical sides have framed racking panels with steel pins and tilted adapters that use indirect lighting to illuminate the structure from behind. The back wall has a steel-cable diamond module for display and bottom wood cabinetry that has been lacquered in gray to keep the modern look. A cooling unit is hidden behind the perforated technical ceiling with high hats.

North Miami Wine Room Island

Miami, Florida

This piece is the main focal point in the home. A short back wall has been used to place the TV and act as a support for the white wooden soffit. Placing equipment and having this decorative walk-in island that separates the main living room was a prime structural challenge. Clean white-lacquered metal wine racks and bottom cabinet allow for bottles to be placed in various forms and create an elegant ambiance by utilizing the colorful RGB LEDs.

Matisse Corner Wine Room

Delray Beach, Florida

Pictured is a glass-enclosed wine room situated in a corner room next to the entrance of the home. The two glass sides achieve an aesthetical view from various angles of the displayed wine. The dark-lacquered metal racking is combined and alternated with acrylic shelves so that the wine can play more of a protagonist role. A glass counter next to one of the walls has been placed to display special bottles.

Belmonte Wine Room

Valdemorillo, Madrid, Spain

An underground wine room with extensive capacity was designed to display bottles in a variety of racks and positions. This was the first project to incorporate a central diamond module with steel rods, perimeter lighting, large side panels with steel pegs, and tilted adapters. This hardware is placed against a lacquered MDF panel as well as the bottom cabinetry. Impressive RGB spotlights are used for a special glow.

Zagaleta Refrigerated Wine Room

Marbella, Malaga, Spain

A large glass-enclosed wine room designed for a new luxury home provides the best in aesthetics as well as functionality to both store and access wine. Two fridges are embedded into the back wall, allowing white wine to be ready at serving temperature. Modern metal racking was done in shelves as well as diamond niches that were coupled with an open-concept bottom cabinet for special wine crates and magnums.

Fan Palm Wine Room

Boca Raton, Florida

A centered refrigerated wine room is placed against a large living room wall. To situate the cooling unit and not hamper any ceiling molding, an insulated wood soffit was placed at the right height from which the glass enclosure would wrap around. This piece has enough depth for a walk-in and includes laser-cut metal racking with a tasting counter as well as an innovative bottom cabinet with a real stone veneer counter for warmth.

Rhodes Corner Wine Room

Delray Beach, Florida

This new home construction has a glass-enclosed wine room placed in the corner of their entertainment room. It provides a practical location to access wine for guests, yet its lighting solution provides for an incredible look. Its finishes in wood and gold match the décor perfectly. A window to their hallway—with separate lighting, acrylic, and cables pieces—makes this design special from both of its two sides.

Stone Tile Wine Room

Stuart, Florida

Our design focuses on providing a very clean and elegant look in this modern home. Low-iron glass enclosure, white stone tile, light gray and thin metal racking, and acrylic pieces superbly reflect the LED lighting placed throughout. Just enough red wine bottles provide an addition of aesthetics. The tasting counter and front acrylic display element also add an alluring feature for a superior dining-room ambiance.

Windward Wine Enjoyment Room

Jupiter, Florida

A new racking design was placed in this dining room. This area was converted from a more sit-down formal area to a place to taste and enjoy wine at leisure. It is accompanied by a custom counter-height table and matching stools. The space is perfectly lit and is very elegant with clear-painted metal and acrylic racking that dynamically positions the bottles. All finishes match other elements in the home décor.

Mariposa Wine Wall

Palm Beach Gardens, Florida

A refrigerated wine wall in the dining area is embedded into the wall with glass doors to view and access the wines. Side mirrors provide an infinity view and a lovely visual effect. Wine racks alternate shelving in laser-cut metal and acrylic while tensed-steel cables display bottles in numerous ways. The bottom wood cabinet allows for additional storage as well as for wine crates to be placed. The lighting provides a classy glow.

Plantation Spider Wine Wall

Palm Beach Gardens, Florida

A unique corner wine wall that incorporates a special "spider" design is utilized for the best wine display. Lacquered, thin metal framing—using only acrylic and glass shelving for a total floating effect—gives this piece a dynamic look. Added unique features include a lighted humidor, drawers, a lighted tasting counter, and an acrylic glass holder with a custom laser-cut designed stool. Mixing gold and white finishes gives this project an inspired look.

Sunrise Wine Wall and Bar Divider

Coral Gables, Florida

A glass-enclosed refrigerated wine wall and serving-bar space has been placed to separate the kitchen and living room areas. This element includes a drop-down soffit to integrate with the rest of the ceiling features and provides a thin metal structure with glass and acrylic to see right through. The lighter bar counter, glass holder, shelves, and drawer make this combination not only aesthetical but also practical.

V

B

A
L-
wa
co
to
gl
co

L

N

A
me
sid
an
pla
wi

Transitional Home Projects

Ponce Wine Enjoyment Room

Coral Gables, Florida

Pictured is a unique refrigerated wine room that provides a place to select, open, and taste wine on a central table, which features backlit white glass and an acrylic-glass holder resting above. This room is complemented with a lighted cigar humidor and a display window where featured bottles can be displayed and seen even outside the room. Warm materials that can be highlighted with varying RGB LED colors create this exclusive glow.

Bridge's Corner Wine Room

Boca Raton, Florida

A corner refrigerated dining room has been placed in order to feature the maximum visibility of wine in this dynamic configuration. Dark metal and wood elements are accompanied by glass and acrylic to create a special contrast with the white LED-lighted wall. Warm colors are used to provide a transitional look. It is complemented with a custom ladder and upper magnum display shelves as well as a perforated, technical wood ceiling.

West Lake Wine Tasting Room

Fort Lauderdale, Florida

Here is a transitional design for a wine room that perfectly mixes wooden wall panels and light, tensed-steel cables with lacquered metal hooks and cabinetry. The perimeter's warm white lights provide a particular glow, displaying wine with bottle's neck out, on their side, and even on the wooden counter. Although refrigerated, there are a couple of sofa chairs and a small table for a quick tasting and an overall recreational experience.

DJ Khaled Wine Display Rooms

Miami Beach, Florida

Shown are twin refrigerated wine rooms with different temperatures that highlight wine as well as spirits. This piece is placed in between a waterfall using a "spider" racking design for a notable look. Glass-enclosed spaces with racking in the back, mostly in acrylic shelves with glass shelving on the sides, are utilized for added display. For this project, a custom wave-slat ceiling solution was used. Additionally placed is a unique custom stool and a lighted cigar humidor.

Emerson Wine Room

PARKLAND, FLORIDA

Pictured is a complex understairs curved closet that has been converted to a wine room with many distinct features. Racking was developed in metal framing primarily but warmed up with wooden slats in front of the joints, ceiling cover, and bottom cabinet. Included is a lighted tasting counter, a glass holder, a cigar humidor, and a wine fridge with the ideal serving temperature for white wine. This is a great space to select, open, and taste wine with friends.

Leafy Wine Room

Coral Gables, Florida

A glass-enclosed area has been placed against a small side wall to be seen from the entrance hallway as well as the den. There was a vital design feature that attributes black framing for the basis of contrast on the enclosure hardware as well as the wine racks. The shelving holding the bottles was all done in acrylic for transparency. The racking (three bottles deep) allows for added storage by utilizing space for any crates below.

Mariner Wine Room

Jupiter, Florida

A large and unique room placed at the home's entrance highlights these bottles in a fashionable way. Big wooden columns support glass fronts on four sides with elegant and light acrylic racks and steel cables. In the center, special adapters tilt bottles so that they can be viewed equally on both sides. Added warmth is achieved with a lighted humidor and a wood-slat ceiling to cover any equipment. The unique LED glow is reflected evenly by the acrylic pieces.

Los Pinos Wine Room and Tasting Area

Punta Cana, Dominican Republic

This refrigerated wine room with a warm, unique feature utilizes a volcanic stone wall and glass sides so that the wine can be seen from both inside and outside. Modern racking with light steel, cables, and acrylic allows visibility and is complemented by an affable glow using vertical LED strips. A very thin display rack placed against the stone and a center tasting table completes this room by storing its spirits and serving as a workstation.

Panel Racks Wine Room

Pinecrest, Florida

This front-glass wine room focuses on integrating the transitional design of the home. To keep with the warm materials, racking panels alternate between gray wood veneer and metallic finishes. Bottles are placed two deep on shelves with various tilted adapters. The bottom cabinet and counter provide extra storage and a place to open wine. Added warmth is achieved with indirect perimeter lighting of the panels.

Elevator Wine Room

DORAL, FLORIDA

The elevator opening had initially been and eventually was conditioned for a small-yet-complete wine room with many unique features throughout. This centrally located project is an integral part of the first floor décor. A tasting counter with drawers, a glass holder, bottom wood cabinet, and technical ceiling are all lit by warm white LEDs. This clean and dynamic space to display, care for, and open bottles provides both a distinctive view and an overall enhanced experience for wine merriment.

Fisher Combined Wine Wall and Room

Fisher Island, Florida

This large wine wall that continues into the wine room was designed to integrate with the rest of the home décor. The racking was adapted for single- and double-deep metal racks lacquered in the same finish as the walls. The wood elements—such as bottom cabinets, tasting counter, and ceiling—even matches other furniture. This project stands as a very clean and elegant solution in highlighting the bottles with pleasant LED lighting.

La Moraleja Wine Enjoyment Room

Madrid, Spain

An underground wine cellar has been constructed to display, store, and enjoy wine while being immersed in a unique and completely furnished space. An exclusive backlit tasting table, wood crate cabinet, bar, and lighted display boxes provide an immaculate place to enjoy wine. The wine is in a refrigerated, glass-enclosed room, easily seen and cared for using a mix of metal and wood pieces throughout.

Marsh Wine Room

Palm Beach Gardens, Florida

This closet has been converted into a wine room to store various bottles and offer a place to open and taste wine. Modern, light gray metal arranges wine in numerous positions. A beautiful, lighted tasting island with a transparent leg and drawer stands in the center of the room. Above is a wooden-slat ceiling that covers the fan coil and allows for correct air circulation. Colorful RGB LEDs provide that spectacular glow.

Transitional Wine Room and Refrigerated Wine Wall

Pinecrest, Florida

The owner requested an unrefrigerated space to enjoy wine in an informal sit-down room with a comfortable temperature. He also wanted to complement it with a cooled wine wall for his own special wine. A transitional design was developed with two-tone metal racks (rust and gray) for an ideal bottle display. Décor and brick walls were added with warm amber LEDs that continue to provide the warmth desired alongside a cozy atmosphere.

Hoyarrasa Transitional Metal Wine Room

La Moraleja, Madrid, Spain

This two-sided glass wine room integrates perfectly in its rustic basement, complete with wood beams, arches, brick walls, and ceramic tile. The lightness of this all-metal racking in a lacquered rust tone with warm white LEDs gives the protagonist role to the wine and warmth themselves. The dynamic setup allows for bottles of many formats and crates to be ideally displayed toward both the front and back.

Steve Transitional Wine Room

Fort Lauderdale, Florida

This glass-enclosed wine room was created in a dining area with a more traditional focus on wood and arch features. The enclosure had the challenge to extend out past recessed niches so the space could be a walk-in. Although all racking material was metal, the finish selected was with a texturized rust paint, and the lighting selected would only be a warm white tone so cozy ambiance could be maintained.

Twin Transitional Wine Rooms

Coral Gables, Florida

Two corner spaces were conditioned for symmetrical refrigerated wine rooms. A focus on design kept them warm, transitional, and integrated with the rest of the décor. The small walk-in units have a variety of rust-finished metal shelves accompanied with veneered wood pieces. The bottles displayed tilt toward the outside of the enclosure as well as on their side for the ease of seeing the labels and finding the wine at hand.

Hammock Transitional Wine Room and Bar

Coral Gables, Florida

This house underwent major reforms to its layout and required the living area to incorporate both a wine room and a functional wine bar area. This project is a glass-enclosed room with a mix of lacquered metal racks, tensed-steel cables with hooks, and an open-concept bottom cabinet for crates. This focal point is complemented with a wooden bar cabinet with a lighted tasting counter and glass shelves to add decanters and special bottles.

Ocean Boulevard Wine Room and Counter

Ocean Ridge, Florida

This project was an engineering challenge. It required closing up and adapting an outside space with a spiral staircase to segue into a terrace that leads to a walk-in wine room—and had to be completed with the view to the living room. The U-shaped layout of the racks, mostly metal and acrylic, have their shelving overhung for lightness. The large wooden cabinet has a lighted tasting counter and a cigar humidor that serves as a perfect place to open and decant wines. The project was soon finished with the signature glow, as shown.

Back Wine Wall

North Miami Beach, Florida

The back wall of this room with a central stone table was conditioned with a wine wall from side to side. Its purpose is to ensure a good capacity to display all of the owner's wine in modern racking. This clean, glass-enclosed space allows for a future tasting counter on the left and serves as an ideal location while enjoying wine with friends. The LED lighting creates a warm and cozy environment for all.

Bay Road Wine Display Wall

Miami Beach, Florida

The unrefrigerated wine display wall seen here was converted from a simple arched opening. Squared-off space and dark-perimeter molding resulted in an elegant design that contrasts light- and dark-colored metal. A tall, black-veneered cabinet for storage was added. The utilized wood is matched to the dining table for perfect integration. Frameless glass doors provide a clear view coupled with a warm white lighting of space.

Lake Way Wine Wall and Cabinetry

Palm Beach, Florida

The complete side of this dining room is used to hold a glass-enclosed refrigerated wine wall and its cabinetry. The green finish is used throughout the rest of the room for a total integration of style. The cabinets are placed from floor to ceiling and have doors with both shelves and bottom drawers. The racks consist of clean acrylic hooks, complemented by a light gray metal framing. The upper soffit was also done in MDF to house any equipment.

Modern Condo Projects

Regalia Condo Wine Room

Sunny Isles, Florida

This dining room's wine-wall unit has been placed to provide a special recreational environment. A laser-cut metal racking system with side glass shelves and a central diamond-cable display unit allows bottles to be shown in various positions. The refrigeration unit is placed in a recessed soffit to give this piece a clean enclosure look. By keeping the wall white, the reflection of the LEDs provides a complete gleam.

Porsche Design I Wine Wall

Sunny Isles, Florida

A strategically located wine wall with an emphasis on display, the bottles are placed sideways on acrylic hooks with cables to appear floating, creating an effect that can be viewed from the entire condo. Glass shelves holding unique wine and spirits are clearly highlighted. The cigar needs of this client were met by integrating two small humidors. Lacquered-wood cabinets can be used for storage for both large format bottles and special crates. Warm white LEDs are also utilized in this snug atmosphere.

Claudio Coello Hook Design Wine Room

Madrid, Spain

This was the first cable and hook racking design developed for a condo wine room. The clean and modern look has bottles neck out and on their side, utilizing lacquered metal hooks with tensed cables. The side shelves and the open bottom cabinet provide additional storage for large format bottles as well as special wooden crates. The lighting and gorgeous view creates an unparalleled place to enjoy one's wine.

Ocean Dining Room Wine Wall

Boca Raton, Florida

This beautiful, backlit onyx wall is integrated with tensed-steel cable racks that have acrylic hooks for a transparent and buoyant effect. A linear and symmetrical configuration provides elegance as well as a matchless wine tasting and dining experience. Refrigerated via a remote-ducted system to avoid unnecessary noise or depth, this project's main focus is both ambiance and display in the places where capacity is not an issue.

Porsche Design Tall Wine Wall

Sunny Isles, Florida

This piece was an intensive research and development project that resulted in a wine wall system that could hold the tension of hook racks with bottles of up to sixteen feet. Elegant positioning of bottles neck out and on their side that are two bottles deep are placed in front of a texturized wallpaper. Half the unit is refrigerated and separated with a transparent polycarbonate sheet. This style held a major emphasis on display, elegance, and the work of art in this luxurious condo setting.

LOUIS VUITTON

Porsche Design Wine Display

Sunny Isles, Florida

This project consisted of creating a small-yet-ideally-located unrefrigerated display wine wall. Clear, tempered glass allows for an easy view of wine, and the mirror placed provides a sensation of added depth. Bottles (only one bottle deep) are placed on alternating laser-cut acrylic shelves with steel cables. Perimeter LED lighting in warm white coloring gives the warmth the owner was initially missing. The view of this element can even be seen from the upper floor.

Ortega y Gasset Wine Display Wall

MADRID, SPAIN

This piece also consisted of an extensive research and development project that ended up requiring the placement of a very narrow wine wall in the dining room. Afterward it was ensured that the table was correctly centered and that the doors could be opened. A static cooling coil was placed in an MDF soffit with minimum depth while three glass swinging doors allow a clear view of the beautiful racking. A centered steel-cable diamond module with side panels and steel pegs along with the bottom cabinets are lit to create its colorful and cheery setting.

Transitional Condo Projects

Ritz Carlton Warm Wine Room

Sunny Isles, Florida

This project consists of a corner refrigerated wine room with a glass enclosure and a side entrance door. There is a clear view of the inside wood shelving and its cabinets. Positioning of tensed-steel cables with rust-finished hooks allow two bottles deep to be placed. Cable racking permits transparency, and LED warm-white light placed throughout enhances the ambiance. The ceiling has veneered, perforated panels as well for proper cooled air flow. There is a large emphasis on a transitional focus for this design.

Fendi Mirrored Wine Wall

Surfside, Florida

Pictured is a refrigerated wine wall with a transitional design that mixes wood and rust metal materials with tubes supporting wine. A framed, insulated enclosure has been completed in a brown finish that provides a cozy ambiance when coupled with the warm white LEDs placed on the sides alongside the dark red wine bottles. To get a better visual effect, the back wall has mirrors in place for a crisp reflection and a sense of depth.

Penthouse Transitional Wine Room

Santo Domingo, Dominican Republic

This large wine room was installed in a condo that required traditional wood finishes. Besides the warmth of the material and LEDs, an innovative placement of rust metal and even acrylic pieces creates a most unique design. A tasting counter and ample space allow the owner to select and open wine, display bottles in various positions, and access any elevated ones using a custom metal ladder.

GAJA
PAOLO SCAVINO
CONTERNO
BAROLO
Chateau Pavie
SOLAIA

Pintor Rosales Wine Wall

Madrid, Spain

This project consists of a unique wine wall that was created with a transitional focus and that places wood paneling on the back and side to match the finishes in the nearby kitchen. A custom lighted humidor is attached to the back with bottles surrounding it. The equipment for cooling and humidity is hidden in the ceiling above. Strategically placed RGB LED strips provide the warm and uniform look that the owner was originally looking for.

Caracas Steel and Wood Wine Wall

Caracas, Venezuela

Showcased is a unique design that was originally created to work alongside the architect Jose Luis Sanchez in order to provide the condo homeowner a unique and modern racking solution with stainless-steel backing and pegs. This has been done with warm wood paneling and framing. It posed an engineering challenge to find the right ducted cooling system and to find a way to develop the unique door hardware so that sealing gaskets would not be needed. The main focus for this piece centers around display and design.

South Ocean Wine Cabinet

Boca Raton, Florida

A new concept, seen here, of a custom refrigerated wine cabinet provides the ease of installing a visual, refrigerated cabinet without the hassle of construction. This is a plug-and-play solution that mixes the expertise of a local cabinet manufacturer with cooling and opening the front and sides in glass and inserting special acrylic racking. LEDs are placed inside, giving an impressive display that is radically different from any other standard wine fridges.

Monad Custom Wine Cabinet

Miami Beach, Florida

A custom refrigerated cabinet was made for a client that wanted to care for his wine without all the construction and permitting that would be needed. This solution only required a standard outlet and was perfect to place in this condo. Bottles are clearly displayed through both front and side glass panels with acrylic racking and LEDs. The floating effect gives an added touch of class to the space provided.

Commercial Projects

Restaurants have been storing their wines both in specialized fridges and in wine cellars/rooms for many years now. This is done so that the wines can be kept at the proper temperature. The importance of their care has always been at the forefront. Being able to keep their inventory for longer periods of time so it doesn't mature ahead of time is crucial. The worst thing that can happen is that these valuable assets are returned by the customers.

The location of these elements can vary, from being close to the dining area for ease of access to even in the backroom where visibility is not perhaps a priority, but it is ensured that they are still well cared for. Besides location, the actual practicality of the wine room is becoming more and more important. Wine racking has evolved in its purpose from once simply holding the wine bottles into making sure that the wine can be placed in an organized and quickly retrievable way. The number of bottles per reference—such as wine region, grape varietal, country, and exclusivity—are all factors to consider when grouping wine and selecting an adequate racking system for it. The wall or room becomes a useful tool for the waiter or sommelier. The more importance a restaurant gives to their wine list and their qualified personnel, the more they should be invested in this unique space and its utility.

The usefulness of the wine cellar/wall is clear, but it is the aesthetics that have just recently garnered importance. Not only is it crucial to have an ample and prestigious wine list, but it is equally important for these bottles to be closer to the customer. Having a glass enclosed wine wall/room serves many purposes. You want the wine to be displayed so it is easy to see what is available and to give the right signal that the wine is properly cared for. Its very presence in the entrance or dining area creates an ambiance that results in it becoming a key focal point. With this basis, restaurants are spending more and more money to evolve from the standard modular racks to those made custom, using materials and finishes in the design of the locale. This, complemented with special lighting, will have customers requesting to sit by this special place in similarity to someone requesting a table with an ocean view. Sales will always be positively affected by the care and quality preserved by these types of projects.

ARZUAGA

Modern Commercial Projects

Restaurant El Bohio

Illescas, Toledo, Spain

This project involves a Michelin-rated restaurant that is managed by Chef Pepe Rodríguez Rey, the main judge in Spain's *MasterChef* program. He wanted a special dining room to highlight his many unique bottles and create an extraordinary dining experience. A highly custom and complex metal racking system was developed to provide various forms of organizing and displaying wine. These bottles were placed in a L-shaped layout, refrigerated glass structure.

Mentidero & Gin Restaurant

Madrid, Spain

This central three-sided glass-enclosed wine room provides an elegant dining experience in this lounge area. This job presented its own set of challenges: the room has a curved ceiling from a garage, but the space had to be completely square, posing as an initial concern that was later. remedied. A cooling unit is fit in the soffit. A new, conceptual metal wine rack with perforated panels and tilted squares allows for an easy view of all the wines that the venue has to offer.

Hotel Princesa Parc

Arinsal, Andorra

This hotel in the principality of Andorra reigns deep in the mountains and has a glass-enclosed wine room in the main dining area for access to wine and a soothing ambiance. The racking is done mostly with lacquered gray metal shelving, framing, and triangular niches plus a tensed-steel diamond module in the center that highlights special bottles. The bottom MDF cabinet is a darker tone of gray and can be utilized for additional storage.

Amparito Roca Restaurant

Madrid, Spain

A restaurant that started in Guadalajara twenty-two years ago and has been in Madrid since 2016, it is famous for its luxury Spanish and Mediterranean cuisine. The wine room was placed in a corner of the dining area so that its select wine references could easily be viewed by their customers. Metal racking is focused to include wine both on its side and tilted. Its tall glass enclosure and lighting provides an ideal dining setting.

Restaurant Fortuny

Madrid, Spain

This emblematic restaurant has a reserved dining area on its second floor that requires wine to be placed in two refrigerated niches. The fixed-glass glass enclosure on the dining side has swinging doors to allow easy access for the waiters. The warm ambiance created with brown metal finishes and LEDs makes this dining experience one of a kind.

Restaurant Romano

La Moraleja, Madrid, Spain

A beautifully designed Italian restaurant in an affluent community north of Madrid incorporates a modern wine wall at the entrance. An important challenge was placing this unit in a very narrow wall next to a stairway. A special cooling equipment had to be sourced and configured for proper air circulation. The lacquered racking and lighting provides an ideal display for wine and a distinctive ambiance.

Restaurant Alabaster

Madrid, Spain

Located in the center of Madrid, this restaurant is famous for its modern Gallego cuisine with an emphasis on seafood. It belongs to a group that holds Michelin Star recognition. The corner glass-enclosed wine room provides the entire dining area with an elegant view of their very exclusive wines. The references are organized in square and triangular lacquered metal niches with bottom cabinets that are used for crates.

Transitional Commercial Projects

Restaurant Bibo

Madrid, Spain

Showcased are unique wooden wine racks for the Michelin-rated chef Dani Garcia. The design was worked on alongside prestigious designer Lazaro Rosa-Violán. Space is organized with wood niches as well as unique diagonal dividers in the bottom cabinet, complete with brass inlays, for wine to be served from. The end of the corridor has a mirrored wall to give a sense of continuity. LEDs throughout give the space its warmth and cozy atmosphere.

Restaurant Ten con Ten

Madrid, Spain

This restaurant is one of the most popular places to go to eat and have drinks in Madrid. The restaurant needed two outside wine-display units next to their dining area and one large storage room for over 2,500 bottles. The twin units allow wine to be viewed by clients for their selection while contributing to the environment's cozy atmosphere. The main room had complex metal engineering racks developed to allow organization and to easily access the bottles.

Wine Wave Tasting Area

Delray Beach, Florida

This was the first wine racking project by Dragon Cellars in the US. A conditioned upper-floor area for tasting events utilizes light gray metal racks that clearly show labels, contains space for TV presentations, and even has lower cabinetry to store extra wine. This main wall is complemented by another counter and has similar racks on the side. The ambiance creates a snug environment for guests to relish a notable wine escapade.

Otto Restaurant

Madrid, Spain

A tall and warm-looking wine room has been placed at the entrance of this restaurant and lounge. A new racking system with veneered natural stone panels that has been backlit with steel rods allows wine to be placed in various positions. Upper wood-perimeter lit boxes are used for the display of large-format bottles. A golden metal ladder with glass shelving creates a unique ambiance that integrates with the rest of the warm-element designs.

Restaurant Asador Esparteras

Toledo, Spain

A refrigerated wine room has been placed in the entrance of this restaurant. This project's prime focus is to care for and serve wine to the customers, acting as a display to sell special wine and spirits. Lacquered metal racks with laser-cut shelves, a central worktable in wood, and a glass display counter provide an ideal place to hold the "Third Best Wine Collection in Spain," resulting in an increase of the owner's sales.

Restaurant Estay

Madrid, Spain

A transitional wine room and wall was placed to care for and display wine in this emblematic Madrid locale. The glass enclosure was done to form a display arch, followed by a room that can be entered from the bar side. To provide the warmth and transparency the owner was looking for, rust metal and glass pieces are utilized alongside warm white LEDs. This results in a prime focal point for the restaurant.

Alborada Wine and Spirits Store

La Coruña, Spain

This special locale that sells and serves top wines and spirits was added to the Michelin-rated Alborada Restaurant. This large space was designed to provide a variety of displays in warm materials, finishes, and lighting. Rust-lacquered steel with pegs, laser-cut niches for spirits, and a separated wood divider for added wine provide the ideal setting to browse, taste, and select quality bottles to bring home.

Restaurant Señorio de Alcocer

Madrid, Spain

Pictured is a Spanish restaurant that values an emphasis on their meat and wood-grill oven. They had a ground floor corner used for storage converted into a beautiful, refrigerated wine room. The space was soon optimized. Besides storage, its main purpose became to exhibit the wines for customers' selection. Two-tone, laser-cut metal racking has placed bottles on their side, neck out and tilted for optimal viewing. LEDs provides the needed refreshing ambiance.

Restaurant Asador Donostiarra

Madrid, Spain

This famous Basque grill restaurant was established in 1974 and has since been visited by many sports and social celebrities. Their main dining area has its ambiance enhanced with a unique wine room with metal tubes and support pegs lacquered in the same color as the stone to give the bottles their floating effect. This locale also has a private dining room with a glass window, showcasing wine displayed on steel cables and hooks.

Hotel Val de Neu

Baqueira, Lleida, Spain

A renowned ski resort's five star GL Hotel in the Pyrenees mountains requested a placement of a fully glass-enclosed wine room. This space is perfect in separating the dining area, displaying the wine from their list as well as allowing accessibility for the waiters. Very light, metal, rust-finished and laser-cut racks allow for an ease of view and organization of all types of bottles and wine crates. Warm white LEDs help with the integration of the wood décor.

El Bocaito Restaurant

Madrid, Spain

Photographed is a 1966 established classic Andalusian restaurant popular for their southern cuisine and tapas. They have numerous photos of famous guests visiting this locale. This piece was done by converting it from a small wooden shelving area to a metal refrigerated wine cabinet. To ensure a nice fit with the warm ambiance, metal racking and the exterior was done in a rust finish. Their emblematic dog logo pulling on their name was even carefully laser cut on top.

Restaurant El Lago de Boadilla

Boadilla del Monte, Madrid, Spain

This restaurant located by an emblematic lake focuses on traditional Spanish and Mediterranean cuisine. A very light wine room is enclosed in glass, and upper wood soffit houses the cooling system. A walk-in focus allows waiters access to wines that are placed in lacquered metal racks in varied positions. This also provides customers an ideal view and special glow attained by the LED lighting customizations.

Innovative Renders

There is no limit to what the mind can create. A designer, even of wine cellars, has the ability to envision new ways of organizing and displaying wine that are both novel and refreshing. Wine racking can, at times, become standardized and have very little innovation behind it. When new ideas do come up, the best way to visualize these is to do realistic renders. Before the actual system is put into production, being able to see how these racks will look ensures that the aesthetics are right on track and helps establish the potential clients that are willing to purchase it. This is not always applied, especially to owners who have a very good spatial visualization of 2D drawings. Besides being great tools for new creations, they ensure that the final project can be seen ahead of time for systems that were utilized in the past. The comparison of what was proposed and what actually results can be uncanny. There are some comparison examples in this book that are difficult to tell which one is real and which is not. It's surprising how similar both representations are.

CYNTHIA ROMÁN
DISEÑO DE INTERIORES

Next-Generation Modular Rack

Dragon Cellars has focused on only producing 100 percent custom wine cellars over the years. This means that there have never been any wine racks in stock and that each project is created from scratch. The company strategy has allowed us to evolve into the most creative, luxury-oriented wine cellar designers for our clients (even the most demanding ones) in the market today. Our motto of "Exclusive designs for unique people" is a clear summation of this philosophy.

With this level of expertise on the unlimited ways of displaying and organizing wine in various types of materials, finishes, and looks, this can very well be applied to the world of modular racking systems. As a way to help the company evolve, it makes sense to participate in this type of transforming market and accompany other systems that have been around for some time. There is a growing demand for wine racks that have standard features and can be adapted to spaces depending on the available dimensions. Considering what is currently available, Dragon Cellars has created a modular system that stands out from others and is beyond versatile with its variety of possible configurations. The logistics of this new focus (patent 11425997) is still ongoing, but we have decided to share some of its characteristics, drawings, and photos with you in this book.

Main characteristics:

- A variety of configurations and forms for storing and displaying wine.
- Finishes provide solutions for modern and transitional designs.
- LED strips and component housing are optional and can be added on later.
- Shelving (acrylic and metal) can hold a variety of accessories for better organization and display.
- Racking structure can be divided in two vertical pieces to facilitate packaging.
- Shelving can be separated to accommodate both standard- and large-format bottles.
- Bottom and top shelves can position various wine crates.
- Special acrylic adapters with cables can be used for neck-out or sideways-displayed wines.
- Complements anything that is in the modular-racking market.
- Vertical modules done in single- and double-wide dimensions to provide versatility.

BOTELLERO MODULAR V3
COMPOSICION TIPO 1
BANDEJA ARAÑA
2 BOTELLAS LATERAL

BOTELLERO MODULAR V3
COMPOSICION TIPO 2
BANDEJA ARANA
2 BOTELLAS FRONTAL

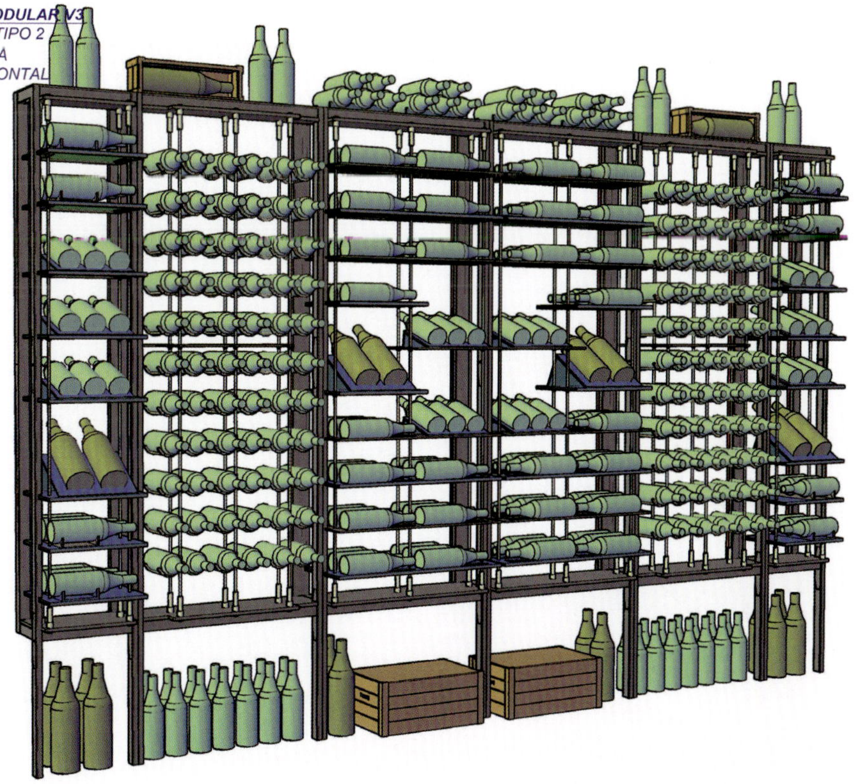

Collaborations and Gratitude

The creativity applied to making these projects a reality, although stemming from me as master designer, is supplemented from a wide variety of sources. The involvement of the Dragon Cellars owner and their interior designers provides very useful guidance so that the finished product is not only functional but also aesthetic and ensures a perfect integration with the rest of the home. The custom manufacturing capability in Madrid, Spain, makes certain that all elements are done to the highest quality and fits in the designated space before transporting. The local contractors are essential so that the spaces are properly prepared, equipped, assembled, and executed.

It is impossible to acknowledge all the contributors in these years of operation, but I would like to specially recognize:

- Marisol Lecuna, General Manager of Dragon Cellars
- Juan José Perez, Director of Fabrication and Dragon Cellars Spain Manager
- Gregorio Moya, Director of Greja Electroclima in Madrid
- Aurora Murillo, Project Director of Dragon Cellars
- Alvaro Yanguas, APT Construction President
- Gene Valdini, GPN Construction, President
- Ed Sasso, EDS Refrigeration, President
- Javier Orta, Blue Tech Refrigeration, Director
- Roger Ochoa, RO Projects Glass Installer, Owner

To my publisher, Brown Books Publishing Group, thank you for helping me make this book a reality. Milli Brown, Brittany Griffiths, Carissa Demma, Sterling Hooker, and Danny Whitworth all put in their hard work on the project. And to all others, our most sincere appreciation. We hope to continue to collaborate in the future!

About the Author

Alberto (Al) Fuentes is the president, master designer, and consultant of Dragon Cellars. He has been dedicated to making this unique company a success, culminating in seventeen years of providing demanding clients the most innovative luxury wine cellars and related furniture in the market. His projects have been sold in over seven countries, with more to come!

Al was born in New York City in 1960 to immigrant parents from La Coruña, Spain. He lived back and forth between the US and Spain in his childhood and young adulthood, where he served as a US Air Force captain. He joined in 1979 and opted for an early retirement in 1995. During this timeframe, he worked mostly in the aircraft maintenance area, having been stationed in various bases, and left with the position of commander after serving in a training detachment in Georgia.

Returning to Spain with his family as a civilian, he held numerous jobs related to human resources, headhunting, and worked as an associate professor for three universities, teaching over eight subjects in a ten-year span.

In 2007, he decided to start up a company in Madrid for the design, manufacturing, and installing of custom wine cellars, focusing on new and innovative designs in the luxury market. In 2014, the company, Dragon Cellars, was established in Delray Beach, Florida, and has since created works of art for the display, storage, care, and enjoyment of wine in the most exclusive homes and restaurants. Dragon Cellars has completed more than 320 projects.

Al holds an MBA from Albany State University, a master's in aeronautical science, a bachelor's in professional aeronautics from Embry Riddle Aeronautical University, and a powerplant technology associate degree from the Community College of the Air Force.